Reimmersion

Also by Tony Steven Williams
and published by Ginninderra Press
Sun and Moon, Light and Dark

Tony Steven Williams

Reimmersion

for Arlene

Reimmersion
ISBN 978 1 76109 489 7
Copyright © text Tony Steven Williams 2023
Cover image: Tropical Mangroves by Arlene Williams

First published 2023 by
GINNINDERRA PRESS
PO Box 3461 Port Adelaide 5015
www.ginninderrapress.com.au

Contents

Encounters	7
Compromise	9
freedom	11
Trust	12
Elephants on Surfboards	13
Those promises	14
Devolution	15
Encounter	17
nostalgia in a wineglass	18
Early Thanksgiving	20
blend	21
bereavement	22
Waterside memories (sijo)	23
Man of Fire	24
Facebook Ghost	25
Beautiful Man	26
Commuting Beggar	28
Holding the dark down	29
Pendulum	30
90 Minutes	31
Tanka 1	35
Environment	41
Complacency	43
Soon	44
Plus ça change…	45
This Old Road	46
Cézanne, a cat and I	47
Lost in spacetime	50
Space odyssey two thousand and something	51

Branching out	53
Captured	54
Pivot	55
Roos at the bushfire	56
Post inferno	57
Summer-sweet. Summer-bitter.	58
Regrowth	59
Tableau with no background music	60
Water	61
Community	62
Tanka 2	**63**
Earthly and Unearthly	**69**
Planetary conversations: Pluto speaks out	71
Planetary conversations: Gaia (our earth mother gives us some advice)	73
Under the sink	75
Flashback	77
skin blues	79
On Reflection	80
The good thief	82
Planetary conversations: Venus laments	83
Barefoot	85
Flying the colours	86
Slow Summer Night	88
Kandinsky – Composition VII (1913)	90
Rebirth	91
Acknowledgements	93
About the author	94

Encounters

Compromise

Our bridge pierces the void across the river,
        an elaborate brooch on a crinkled blue dress,
dividing river, uniting land. Underneath,

water still flows; at either end the land
        holds still. As I step along the hot walkway,
cooled by a downstream breeze, steel trusses

flicker slowly across my vision, each side
        a magic lantern parade of picturesque frames.
Ahead, my destination focuses more sharply.

Glancing back, sweet sentiment fades,
        but it will always be with me. I'm thinking
that if this bridge were taken down by quake,

tsunami or bad politics, for example, the river
        might fall back to its former self, each shore
isolated: and after a while either skyline

would acquire that dark, distrustful aspect
        that I recall. But we still have this bridge,
two-ways friendly, no border force,

no customs gate. As I reach midpoint, the wind
        is strong but kind, blowing through my hair
like an overactive benediction. I inhale its tang,

let it flood my body. Somewhere, I've read
        that whether beam, arch, suspension, cantilever,
Bailey or girder, the strength of a bridge

is not only ties and cables but also tension
        and compression, stretching and shortening,
the balance between the two. I walk on.

freedom

We all live in cages and cages have bars:
convention, serendipity, heredity, culture,
loosely held in distant shadow, frangipani fresh,
or cold, heavy, cynical, griddle-hard against the face.

We all live in cages and cages have doors:
locked, rusted, forgotten, unloved,
or oiled, shining, swinging free at a fingernail's touch.

No escaping cages – we leave one
to find ourselves inside another.
Cages within cages within cages.

So perhaps freedom is about the biggest cage
– or who can open theirs (or someone else's)
to further sweeten the air.

Trust

It's complicated around here.

All those circles of trust,
floating about, covering our universe,
spinning, intersecting, diverging,
swerving, diving, colliding.

Those circles of trust, they're everywhere;
colours of emotion swirling inside
machine washes of who we are and what we do:

innuendo, rumour, lipstick on a glass,
self-sacrifice, love, altruism, bravery,
betrayal, circumstance, treachery,
promises made, promises kept, promises breached,
spies, lawyers, finance, politics, trade, religion…

Those circles of trust…

Elephants on Surfboards

All those self-appointed Caesars
and Caesarissas with their extravagant
gestures, battle cries of half-truths,
inaccuracies; shouting down those
who dare dissent, exploiting us
with psychology, confusing our minds,
decrying all experts bar minorities
who justify their stance. They've blasted
themselves deaf to nuance,
the world view from their padded bubble
stripped to film noir. White noise washes
over us like perpetual surf. Whatever we say
overruled, disregarded, disrespected –
for they know best what's best for us.

We need to be elephants on surfboards,
thick-skinned, determined, riding
their furious waves right into the beach:
questioning, factual, convincing,
polite elephants, clever elephants,
showing them other worlds
until the more fair-minded listen
 – and we can have a conversation.

Those promises

His aftershave moments of beneficence
scatter from him
like finely shredded magazine gloss
flung into the air
to spin away with the wind
or settle as tiny, coloured piles
tucked into dark corners
for spiders to ponder
or be flushed down a stormwater drain
with other waste
pipe to river to ocean
swallowed in watery wilderness.

Devolution

Such a colourful spirit you were,
full of starbursts, meteor showers,
rainbows spinning inside kaleidoscopes,
a volcano on the run, dummying,
shimmying, eyeballing the universe
to take you on. You transported
me from microscope to telescope,
from beetle to falcon. That was exciting.
That really was!

But now…

What devolutionary process
or reverse alchemy has bleached
you to this sheet of cellophane
on a windowpane? You're married
to the clock, you bigamist!
hip-locked to the situation,
tongue-shackled to your work.

You've polished our lives
beyond reflection: we're slipping
down the gentlest waterslide
inside a cushioned cylinder,
water chuckling beneath blue velvet,
everything accounted, smoothness
mandated to the micron…

We're opposite buds
on a bipartite stem: fire and ice,
chasing suns on alternate horizons.

We're ghosts, passing through
and by each other with barely
an ectoplasmic nod.

Encounter

Deep in the rainforest
where water whispers
down the hillside
to fall into the gorge,
the sounds of centuries
echo still,
and all is subtle shades
of sienna, moss and amber,
where granite tors
raise sundered heads
over jungle tangle,
and fabulous creatures
fly, crawl, hop
or climb the trees
towards the canopy's light.

In this special place
I find you.

Your face ripples beside mine
mirrored in the meniscus
of the quiet rock pool
fringed by grass and bracken.

nostalgia in a wineglass

behind bow
glass windows
shapes
glitter
ghostlike
through
spinning
burgundy

slowly, slowly
images
crystalise…

on the beach
I find you –
vermilion
tank top
pulled in
at the waist
long
pageboy cut
flowing
and whirling
as you laugh

your
Mediterranean
eyes sing
of the sun
ultra-blue
near-violet
teasing me
over a copper
shoulder

wineglass
you shine!

my fingers
enfold
your narrow
waist
as I tilt you
towards me

our
lips
touch

spice
blackcurrant

slowly
passionately
I empty you
into me

Early Thanksgiving

Campfire evening, walls softly seeping, roof patterned in soot. Light-shy bats converse with pendent roots poking through the ceiling, green-tinged. Stars and a full moon spectate through the laughter of the cave's lips. Moths navigate the haze, flutter over a collected guano pile and scattered toys and tools. A sabre-tooth tigress sags over gentle flame. Hard-won from spear and tracking craft, respected, revered, she is reanimated now in the flared nostrils of the celebrants. Freshly picked nuts and fruits pyramid on wooden platters. Juice of fermented berry, rare indeed, held in cups in hands, sipped slowly, savoured. Roasted tubers, honey, fish, water chestnuts, cooked, treated, especially for this day. The man begins to sing, vibrant baritone, the woman a chilling alto. Harmony, goosebump harmony, fills the space. Then the children, best they can. Family songs of hunting and gathering sanctify the cavern, chants of gratitude to the spirits for their survival, not just for now, but in hope for the winter and beyond. It's been a good year, such a good year.

blend

between
she/her
and
he/him

they/them
was born

neither
the wrong
nor right
side
of
the tracks
but
connecting
two rails

bereavement

when losing a loved one
fluid drains from your body
every crevice   organ   internal space
pumped dry
creasing the skin   numbing the mind
an abandoned starfish
tossed high on the sand by an ebbing tide
dry and dizzy in the heat of the sun
there is no known cure   for bereavement
but over time osmosis frequently occurs
sweet recollections filter in
suspended in a supple liquid
honey and light
regrowing your body
approximating its original shape
rehydrating much of the desert

Waterside memories (sijo)

The breeze is soft now. Dying sunlight gilds the lake, its touch limns

my empty glass. A pair of ibis land in the reeds, gathering

glitter in their wake. Wedding photos moisten under my eyes.

Man of Fire

I saw him then and always. Fire-pit eyes,
both glass and true, that flamed the dry sad ward
declaring what his voice could not, that he
would win his war. But he was on death row,

condemned from Trojan gifts of cigarettes
dispensed to boost morale on a distant front.
We'd gather round his bed too long like ghosts –
for what was there to say? Until those coals

of eyes would blaze and his head rotate away.
Dismissed, we'd leave him with his pride complete.
Yet on his final day, with anger waved
aside…perhaps morphine, perhaps belief,

he smiled, reached out a hand for us to hold,
his soldier heart returning from the cold.

Facebook Ghost

You were quite the aficionado, your life laid out as a memoir of colour, text and emoji. But it's been such a long time since your last post – and since the last post was played for you.

I called on you the other day (virtually, that is). Our conversation was necessarily one-sided; but it was wonderful to revisit your pages, to link with you again.

covering old walls
hieroglyphs and paintings
young warriors slain –
such a human trait
disagreeing to agree

Beautiful Man

when tomorrow merges into today
and today becomes yesterday
and the mind has twisted inwards
fixated, unable to think outside
its cranial cage
winding round & around & around
a tormented snake
an ouroboros feasting on its tail

when you know you should re-enter
the world, but cannot
a self-inflicted stubbornness
from a wounded spirit
just you, endless Netflix, bottles of booze
pizza deliveries, the disabled phone

when ennui has spread
its penumbrous wings, and you
sit and mope, wasting the days
like tearing toilet paper from a roll
just for the bloody hell of it
one sheet after another
just for the bitter-sweet
monotony of it, until
there are no more rolls

is that what happened to you
Beautiful Man

perhaps
in your rare social media posts
critiquing SF films
in those times you couldn't be contacted
there were clues we should have read
or you didn't want us to
slouching behind your door, ignoring the gauge
until the oxygen was gone

Commuting Beggar

A battered, straggle-haired man, blazoned blue with tats, boards our free city-loop bus. Eyes on high beam, facing the long, rubbered aisle, he searches for an empty seat. Feet stutter up the centre. A forefinger touches, wraps hard about a post, keeping his body still against the vehicle's jerking. He holds for a while. Sinks into the fabric. Pokers to attention. Zeroes in on the bus's monitor in a glass-glaze stare. Three stops later, he unwinds his whippet-thin body, trudges to the bus door. I imagine him shuffling to a shadowed space beside an illuminated shopfront.

weeds gone to seed
over the garden path –
broken journey

Holding the dark down

She told me she coped by thought-rolling
        any freshly hatched dark between her palms
into a tight sombre ball, thrusting its noir-ness

down, down beyond sunlight's compassion,
        where countless atmospheres of pressure
pounded it with other caliginous detritus

that coated the ocean floor of her mind;
        down, down to where benthos bred
and blackness reigned. She would damn

the dark to the guard of the fanged viperfish
        and the watchful luminescence of anglers
and lanterns, denizens of her submarine

unconscious – that sequestered netherworld
        at the nadir of her existence. She told me
the freshly hatched dark must never mature,

never be allowed to burst to the surface,
        never be permitted to swallow the light
from her new life   into itself.

Pendulum

He is, many would say,
        a possessor
of remarkable luck and favour.

Yet, he's been stepping between shadow and light,
        knees bent, throat exposed
to vagaries and rhythms,

either spiralling down into defiles
        of darkness
that catch and claw in cascades

of thorn and interlock,
        or soaring, hawklike,
on star-bound thermals to glory.

Now, on this jetty, this quiet, moon-hung
        night, his footfalls
softly comment on timeworn planks

that drag behind, accompany, run ahead,
        triangulating
in a blunt point at the jetty's end.

There he can break the thread –
        all those years
of unannounced pendulum and pain.

90 Minutes

On stage at the stadium,
we're sweating an ocean,
backlit, front lit, high lit, downlit,
haloes, rainbows, strobes.
I nail the high B, screaming
through the guitarist's
keening riff, the drummer's
final thump. On cue, the applause
is nuclear; their gift to me
for my gift to them.
30,000 hands wave, the floor
judders beneath our feet.
I raise my arms in benediction.

Was that only two years ago? Was that really me?

My fame crescendoes
through cloud, a skyscraper
departing its foundations,
bound for the stratosphere,
programmed for the sun.
We plunder starstruck nights,
gig after gig, dollars growing,
dollars going, crops under locust.

Was that only last year? Was that really me?

I'm spinning in space,
girls a blurry procession
of one-night delights, the towns
– I forget their names often –
a string of Lego projects.
Oh, my friends,
I have forgotten even you.
How did this singer
become the narrative of those songs
of loneliness and despair
he performs so well?

But it's all survival, high-walking walls
between ecstasy and insanity,
managers and agents chivvying
me along, eyes averted
from the sniffing behind curtains.
They tell me *Keep going!*
Or the next big thing will seize your place!
But it's hard to take off
when you're hanging in air.

What keeps me alive
as the days darken, tunnel in,
is that oh-so-short
grab of heat, light, noise;
that smell of passion;
that shared nirvana;
those glorious 90 minutes
sharing my soul, singing my heart,
when the world stops to listen
and all else is forgotten.

That's the real me. That's who I am.

Tanka 1

I feel the truth
and fiction in your
never committing…
when a half-moon lights the sky
is it waxing or waning?

        all I have
        memories and luggage
        no turning back
        this airplane flies
        in only one direction

our busker
orchestrates the square
guitar case altar
fills with offerings
from bending backs

flotsam –
refugees drift
between tides
a beach in the distance
glistens under stars

        flying far
        a V of shelduck
        new leaders
        refresh the flock –
        pilots swapping seats

an apartment block
tumbles rapidly
to the ground
a sudden archaeology
of family life and loss

rough sleeper
packing case bed
newspaper sheets…
so many stories
beneath their headlines

      clouds of a life
      fall from jetty to sea
      her ashes drift
      on urgent currents
      searching for her husband

long fingers hang
over an empty glass –
seaweed fronds
marooned on rock
hoping for a high tide

Environment

Complacency

generations   decades
years   even months
can trick us into thinking

this is how it is now
and hence ever shall be
then   all turns in a blink

Soon

Deep in a Namibian cavern, huge eggs sit in a cluster as they have for eons. The roar of a lion echoes briefly. Through the jagged mouth of the cave, a waxing gibbous moon faintly illuminates one of the thick black shells.

Many eggs stir, as they do more often now that the years grow warmer, vibrating softly before returning to rest. As each foetus briefly wakes, its brain charges up a little more, sparked by instinctive visions of flight, fire, hunting and gorging. Their growing bodies push ever harder.

it's heating up
hush, tread quietly
don't wake the dragons

Plus ça change…

patterns   shift

yet   always the same

years   of drought

torrents   of rain

forgotten cycles

repeating again

This Old Road

Years of meaningless rain. Black
        clouds and thunder fist the sky
                then slide away like last night's

dream. This old road splutters
        and crumbles under cars that bounce
                and slide over cracks maturing

to trenches. Parachutes of red fog
        plume from rear tyres. This old road,
                no one's friend, as hard and intolerant

as a wronged warrior. Along its edges,
        false green hope from dew and last
                night's scattered droplets. This old road,

all around, wide horizons broken
        by tangles of fence wire coiled high,
                steel tumble weeds caught in roots and dirt.

Occasional white bones surprise the eye,
        a failed homestead pushes up, metal roof
                glinting. Indifferent clumps of mulga

and hardy weed proffer bare subsistence
        for life that forages. This old road ages
                too quickly, suffers often the dispassion

of desert's breath. This old road has lost
        its memory, forgotten how things work.
                But rain *will* come. It will.

Cézanne, a cat and I

In their feline, fearless way, eyes
glare at me from the corner edge
of an apartment roof. The cat,
a tenant playing landlord,
carries those assertive animal colours
of black and white. Sitting upright,
her face tilts forward then down,
a pianist arching to a finale.

Winter-blue day. Cut cucumber fresh.
The views must be vast from the cat's
haughty position, three floors up,
overlooking the lake, the Fountain,
the Carillon, and a languorous flag
atop our politicians' palace.

She appears, though, unmoved
by mere scenery,
perhaps for biological reasons,
since a cat's distance vision
and colour-cone counts are believed
inferior to those of humankind.
But I think it more a feline thing:
You're down there… I'm up here.
I suspect a cat's scope is always shrunk
to prey, territory, safety, the best sun.

Cézanne reduced mountains, people
and oranges to geometric shapes –
artistic building blocks of cylinders,
cones and spheres. If the subject
failed to match Paul's expectations,
his attention inclined to wander.

As I walk around the lake,
merging with cyclists, runners,
strollers, bladers, magpies;
absorbing the privileged scent
of Colombian coffee beans; listening
to the guttural honks of black swans
begging for food; I'm overwhelmed
by the complex vast biospheres
of earth, sky and water, home
to microbes, blue whales –
and creatures like us,
synthetics donors,
planet-wide landscape tailors,
magicians adept at deceits
of creation and disappearance.

I'm envious of that painter and cat,
their world views honed
to cabinet displays; yet, I hope
for wider resolutions, hidden panoramas
beyond lake and mountain.

Nearing walk's end, my inaction
hangs as a heavy yoke of guilt.
I'm a metaphysical novice
caught in a trap, trying to unlock
my hands, my heart, trying to decide
where to be landlord, where to be tenant,
when to construct, when to disassemble.

Lost in spacetime

In an infinity stretching
through cones and folds
beyond our touch
beyond our sight
no centre, no edge
each of us no more than a miniature clock
hurtling through the cosmos
minutely distorting spacetime
(those tick-tock seconds
never return – one wink
and the present is the past)
our proud commentaries
each less than a quark's cackle
with nett zero butterfly effect.

Yet, we are gods on this planet,
hammering, grinding, carving
on our environment, on ourselves
our bellows so loud we don't listen
to those slow harmonies that bind all things.

Like argumentative bees,
we forget to gather nectar. We gorge
on what sweetness exists
then wonder where it went.

Space odyssey two thousand and something

My spacecraft's speed dial display's auto-hovering, redlining near the velocity of light. I'm cheating time, slicing through space in a blunder of stars, galaxies, planets; thumbing my nose at black holes; dodging asteroids; warping; folding; wormholing – whatever tickles Hal 2 (my sentient computer has a strange sense of humour, not altogether displeasing).

This is not all fun you know! I'm ageing Einsteinian slow, and you need shuttle-loads of exercise regimes, hobbies, meditation periods, reading and self-teaching (crosswords and sudoku are just never enough). Maybe I should write that novel I've always dreamed about…

novelty
is difficult to find
in a vacuum

But seriously, I want to see what happens on my return, ten years hence in my time, when – if Hal 2 has worked it right, and she's very boastful but excellent company – my younger brother will be my elder brother while I shall remain (relatively speaking) wrinkle-free. So, in the interim, I'll be dodging all that BS at home: arguments on climate change, dollars, jobs, fossil fuels, trash, rising oceans, epidemics, melting ice, species extinction, atmospheric degeneration.

wolves
many wearing blindfolds
circle the fire

There's a universe of space and time for me to ponder on what it will be like when Hal 2 and I touch down back home. Shall I still need my spacesuit on a Terra not so Firma with blue skies nowhere to be found? Or will it be hallelujah, wisdom and foresight all around? Well, if worst comes to worst, Hal 2 and I will journey on through the cosmos; yup, just the two of us. But I'll miss the beautiful planet.

blue jewel globe
sparkling nervously
in uncertain light

Branching out

Himalayan (or Bhutan) Cypress: *Cupressus torulosa* D.Don
ACT Tree Register: Kingston v1-46 RT0251A

There was a time, in Canberra's formative days,
when Government Printing Office staff
talked family, footy, stamped out cigarettes
in you and your siblings' youthful shade.
Now, there's close to 100 rings assembled
under that intricate bark, and you're branch-by-brick
friendly with these trendy apartments, residents
conversing on balconies, firing up their Webers.
And your foliage has unfolded, a style typical
of your species as that tightly clasped cone
chills out with maturity, gifting light through dark,
sun and moon filtered rather than swallowed.

Indeed, a certain Buddhist hospitality has emerged
in the way your branches span the gaps
(perhaps from your Himalayan heritage!),
rapid transit for pesky possums to scamper
tree-pergola-balcony to smorgasbords of pot plants,
and how you offer meeting stations
for larger birds: gang-gangs, galahs, magpies,
peewees, wattlebirds, currawongs, rosellas…
We watch a sulphur-crested grip an ovoid seed cone
in her claws, cracking the hard-faced, phalanx shields
with her keratin beak, nibbling nutrients. Chirping,
dark eyes fey-wicked, she rips away deep-green,
pine-like needles, clump by clump by clump.

She and we follow their soft, floating voyage
down, gently wilding the footpath, wilding our lives.

Captured

I'm walking in shallows on a sandspit
this gentle morning, shuffling my feet
to awaken hidden stingrays, as you might
in long grass with snakes, to move them on.

A curviform surf is rolling in, parallel barrels
cross the glaze of ocean. Each holds
its shape almost all the way to shore
before rising in a slow-motion arc to reveal

a concave, tattletale window between crest
and sea – a cyan clarity, lit luminous
by midmorning sun, stretching south
to reef, north to headland – before breaking

in an abrupt rinse. I stroll further up the beach,
looking for fishing prospects displaying
inside these windowed waves, and see a shoal
of mullet, two bream and, near the river mouth,

lazy streaks of gar. But, returning for my gear,
the quiet beauty of this bay, gulls wheeling
overhead, dolphins at play, all hold me still;
such a view more than enough to fill my plate.

Pivot

Young boy, homemade slingshot,
stalks through clay dune gullies
under a sloping, eroded cliff.

Stone, rubber, draw, aim, release.
For days he's been unsuccessful,
trying too hard, his prey too fast.

But this time, for the first time,
he feels the unhurried patience
of the predator, a newfound calm.

In range, a juvenile silver gull,
distracted, perched on limestone
above a sunbaking skink.

The boy holds breath and body,
inveigles a stone from his pocket,
stretches the moment.

Stone, rubber, draw, aim, release.
The gull explodes in a bluster
of feathers and dust, tumbles

in a spiralling blur, wing shattered.
Eyes squeeze to weeping slits,
body convulses to stillness.

Young boy, heavy on his haunches,
shining in a sting of sweat and tears,
knows…he cannot do this again.

Roos at the bushfire

Late afternoon in the forest,
rolling, roaring air,
super-dry, crisping hot.
Treetops bend like hair under a drier
on full blast, full heat.
Incandescent reds and yellows strobe
dark rolling eyes. A branch snaps
with a splintered cry –
jumping, brown images fracture
the shallow water of a stream.

A moment of calm as the wind drops.
Shock-still, ears outlined in fire,
necks heaving upwards –
they're sniffing the acid air for escape,
long forgotten the mindless
bounding flight to this strange
terrible place. Undergrowth,
burn control, park management
and politics have no meaning here.

The roos know only that the sun has gone.

Post inferno

The day after evacuation, we're waiting at the base of the hill to return. At last, we're given the all-clear to drive with caution past the barrier and up the looping road ahead. As we ascend, the slope is still alive with smoulder, the occasional split and crack of eucalypt laid low. This burnt-toast smell will linger for weeks. Smoke shades the sun in a sombre midday twilight. Stubborn patches of red flame throb and incandesce on blackened trunks and branches. Sparks pop in multiple short circuits, their weird jigs flickering in our car windows. All those colours, shades, patterns, shapes – danger dressed in nightclub mode – it seems wrong to find beauty here, but we do.

Rounding the corner now, hoping, hoping that the familiar gabled roofline will be unbroken. Our home. Devastation if it's gone, such guilt if we're OK but those around us wiped out…

after the fire
the scent of not knowing
what the future holds

Summer-sweet. Summer-bitter.

There is a painting on my wall of a barn, spanning a hilltop
in the centre of a green paddock, spanning generations,
sun-swept, indomitable, cement floor, metal roof, stone walls,
stacks of pallets, bales of hay, iron implements, sheds abutting
at angles, as solid on the land as clumped coins in a closed fist.

Rolled gold drowses slopes, smoke from a homestead smudges
sky, a fuzz of trunk, leaf and bough hovers on the horizon.
When I last visited, it was the same green and gold of lawn
and hay as in my painting. The same homestead, squatting
comfortably, as if in bark-chewing conversation with cockatoos

that swung and squawled around its veranda poles, the air
summer-sweet, children chiacking, a tractor's rumble,
the buzz of a saw. In the paddock, a different matter. Stubborn
debris and scars lingered, healing slowly like bad surgery,
the owners gradually clearing, preparing to rebuild. Slabs

of concrete, broken, lay like fallen tombstones, wordless epitaphs
to a barn smeared from the farm as a scraper might remove it
from my painting. A massive fireball, they told me, hurled
from the forest, a flaming colossus, wind-enraged, barrelling
through garrotting grey to drop, roar, zero down on the barn,

devouring it as a dragon a dog. A fireball as neatly aimed
as a guided missile on a targeted house, the stored hay
catching alight, a shrieking, howling wind to shatter sanity.
Yet, all around, no collateral damage, spot fires easily dowsed
in the green surrounds. As if the fireball were proving a point.

Regrowth

I'm on the walking track looking out over a lake untidy with debris from the firestorm, but quiet now, recovering beneath a gentle sun. Around its edge, broken contours of blackened trees refract through silver-grey, ash-laden water. A bellbird chimes insistently across the surface. No response. The burnt coconut husk of a boat lies marooned in shoreline mud, Yin and Yang displaying in a strip of untouched paint.

After days of rain, the fire is defeated. I'm so tired, but pure blue sky lifts my head. The air is nectar-sweet with a lingering caramel aftertaste; a deep-breathing gift in the aftershock of numbness, exhaustion, survivor guilt, injury, loss.

under torched bark
epicormic buds
birth green leaves

Tableau with no background music

Odourless ashes commingle
with the dusty floor. A gecko hurries
across mud walls, starshine
falls from a hole in the thatch.
The woman, distended belly,
and the sad bony man wrap
rags around their silent children
(girl and boy). Tomorrow, it is said,
there will be a food drop; tomorrow,
it is said, there will be singing.

Water

water flows or not drowns grows saves floats *water flows or not* clouds rain waterfalls vanish evaporate *water flows or not* inspires cleanses cools quenches *water flows or not* season-to-season mood-through-mood algae-green snow-spray-white ocean-grey *water flows or not* lakes empty rivers flood dams burst glaciers melt tsunamis devastate *water flows or not* birds breed *or not* fish breathe *or not* taps flow *or not* waterholes fill *or not* *water is life or not*

Community

Under blue sky, shading blue water,
orchards of lush green leaves
overflow spindly branches, stems
and roots that appear almost
overwhelmed. The mangroves
straddle and stilt the channels,
their crazy-angled plumbing
embracing the silt, binding the colony,
compartmentalising the brackish
inlet into countless microcosms.
Taking their chance to oxygenate,
pneumatophores, breathing roots,
like giant beds of nails
briefly exposed at this low tide,
spike up from the rotten egg stink
of popping, sucking mud.
But all around, a biodiversity:
crabs, prawns, bream, worms,
jellyfish, mullet, mosquitos, crocs,
nesting birds, fish hatchlings…
Who would destroy a nursery
and a food farm and a community
for pleasure, for profit?

Tanka 2

it's so hard
to shine
find the torch
escape the cave –
a pearl bursts its shell

        roots embrace
        leaves mutter in the breeze
        fearful forest
        battle-drilled, on watch
        for fire, drought and saw

after the earth roared
a child's head and hands
rise through rubble –
an emerging sapling
reaches for sunlight

lantern
I know you are there
on the hill
above my blackness
waiting for me to climb

        how I admire you
        leaning on your cane
        every muscle
        fights for territory
        defying the timelord

aerobics
under the instructor's spell –
dolphins
twist, leap and shine
to the surf's anthemic beat

at the tree's tip
a lone koala nibbles
shrivelled leaves
of red gum distress –
a driver stops, phone in hand

       sails –
       handkerchiefs folded
       just the once
       diagonally
       then blown

wind
cannot blow away
this shadow
I look for sun
to melt its darkness

Earthly and Unearthly

Planetary conversations: Pluto speaks out

I have to say how demoralised
I felt in 2006, when you constructed
those rules for planetary definition,
prematurely bringing in that tricky
third condition* demoting me
to a dwarf planet. *Dwarf planet!*
Such a pejorative term. Such a violation
of planetary rights. You judged
me at your convenience,
without consultation,
when you knew zilch,
considered me a dead pile
of boring, featureless rubble
drifting inside the Kuiper belt
with my good friends Charon,
Styx, Nix, Kerberos and Hydra –
a clear case of guilty
until proven innocent.

But, when that unimpeachable
witness, *New Horizons*, flew
by in July 2015, it found me
geologically remarkable,
complex, contoured,
chockful of phenomena
yet to be uncovered.

And it also discovered,
belatedly, that I have a heart,
Tombaugh Regio, spanning
1,000 kilometres with two lobes
shining bright. A heart of ice,
nitrogen ice, penduluming,
solid to vapour, vapour to solid,
generating retro-winds
against my spin. Not a *lifeless*
heart, but a *pulsing* heart.

Know you this,
that young girl Venetia†
named me well: Pluto,
god of the underworld,
judge of the dead,
and I judge myself
very much alive
you despicable
planet deniers!

The truth is irrefutable.
So, when's the retrial?
the promotion? the apology?
I'm waiting…

---

*IAU (International Astronomical Union): Resolutions for Planet, condition 3: 'It must have cleared the neighbourhood around its orbit'. Pluto is currently regarded as a 'dwarf planet', but there is much dissension.

† Eleven-year-old Venetia Burnley, Oxford, England, 1930.

Planetary conversations: Gaia
(our earth mother gives us some advice)

Modern human. *Homo sapiens.* 'Wise man.'
Now, there's a subject for philosophical debate,
not to mention the gender specificity.
Multidimensional, quasar brilliant, hang-jaw
stupid. That's you. C, O, N, H, P and Ca
with hints of S, K, Cl, Mg and Na to spice up
the mix. All held together by bone, blood,
tissue, ligaments, muscles, organs;
commandeered by brain, nerves, electronics
…an organic machine that's worked
for a paltry 250 ka:* a new-kid, whizz-kid,
0.00025 billion years in and out of Africa.

Must be a tough concept for you, this billion years!
Constrictor-knots the mind,
especially for short-term thinkers
(and you have plenty of those). So, can you survive
another 5 billion years, 200 million constantly
evolving 25-year generations? dodge or detonate
stray meteorites? avoid falling on the self-destruct
button? Can you justify your 'wise' tag?
Because, in 5 billion years, our benefactor the sun,
life giver, very best friend, will be thinking
retirement plans, red giant star plans,
no-longer-including-human plans,
goodbye-to-all-terrestrial-lifeform plans
(won't look so good for me either,
maybe I'll hitch a ride on a passing star).

You will need to be off planet, permanently,
in a distant galaxy, perhaps with ugly,
stereotypical shrunken bodies and 8XL-sized
craniums whizzing around in capsules manufactured
from Neptunian minerals, controlling your crafts
with twitching eyebrows, rotating tongues,
and collective thought transfer.
Too much of your Doctor Who? But yes,
5 billion years is too much to envision.
I suggest go for just six generations:
grandparent, child, grandchild;
grandparent, child, grandchild.
Now you're crystal balling beyond a century,
desperately hoping for rose tints.

* ka: kiloannum, 1,000 years

Under the sink

No escape, no circumvention, no excuses.
Finally, after a plenitude of false promises,
I face this cupboard under the sink
that I must clean, restructure, purify.

Or, there will be consequences…

I drop to bended knees on my Yoga mat,
remind myself, once again,
that every time you delay a task
the monster grows, affects a degree
of difficulty approaching 10.
One day, I swear, one day, I will stop
all this procrastinating procrastination;
this putting off till later
my decision on what to do next.
For you *always* get punished.

I open the doors.
Up front, clean glass jars sparkle
from the kitchen's halogen lights.
They're filled with bottle brushes,
toothbrushes, washing-up brushes.
The kitchen tidy is scrupulously white,
its unsullied lid swings silent
under my touch. Window sprays,
surface sprays, insect sprays, scourers,
sponges, detergents. All neatly stacked.

But, this deep cupboard has shadowy secrets.
Behind the city's crisp veneer lies
its sprawling slum. A hulk, a tumble
of objects, rarely used, crush and smoke
the cupboard's walls and roof,
crowd the plumbing, the basin.
I catch the faint smell of vegetation,
something growing, an impression
of Inca ruins in a jungle thriving
in the humidity from sink and dishwasher.

Perhaps there's an ecosystem there
with small, dangerous, fast creatures
of fur, scale and multiple appendages
scurrying or creeping in the debris,
who will escape if I don't catch them.
They could hide for days in crevice and corner,
waiting for me, one morning, to barefoot
and yawn my way into the kitchen,
waiting to seek venomous vengeance
on the giant being who removed them
from their community,
destroyed their environment.

I pull out the immaculate front row,
assume the position for a little Pranayama,
and prepare to enter my gloved hands
into the unknown.

Or there will be consequences…

Flashback

Quiet pool, the lane to himself. Breathing easy, relaxed, high in the water, shining in a wake of bubbles, his measured kick a metronomic *slappity-splosh*. Each lap, he flips and turns, flotsam pushed into the beach by surf then sucked out by backwash. His mind swims with him, thoughts of family, work, current affairs filtering gently.

20 laps completed, he reaches for the ladder, pulls himself up from the pool.

Now, a faint flicker of déjà vu – strange, blurry, moist images – gone and forgotten, quick as a mayfly's flutter. Perhaps a return visit to amniotic fluid, the umbilical cord his snorkel – or even to when we once emerged, some say, from primordial dampness, a strange, wriggling, large-mouthed, bag-like creature that chose the air.

skin blues

All the rage for us in the 1960s,
that ultra-cool, bronzed look
on anglo/saxon/celtic skin.

Tanning was a competition
between friends; hours spent
under an ambivalent sun,
rotating, grilling
our slow-cooking carcasses
for that winning, even tan,
glowing, healthy-looking
(although we knew the dangers
even then). But for me,
it was all mindless ennui,
denting a beach towel for hours
broken only by quick cool downs
in the surf, reapplying coconut oil,
smudges of zinc cream,
a radio tuned to the top 50,
and a paperback read
at all quarters of bodily revolution.

But for us now,
tanning requires no sun,
no fake magic from a bottle.
We have it for free!
Age spots, liver spots, sunspots,
solar lentigines, lichenoid keratoses
(call them what you like)
covering arms and faces in untidy
brown blotches, increasing over time,
joining up in unstoppable solidarity.

Not quite the look we were after...

On Reflection

I looked in the mirror this morning.
Differently.
Not to search for a bothersome
mole or signs of shaving disaster,
but more as an experiment.

I imagined meeting this man
in the mirror for the first time;
to observe myself as another,
the way other people see me.

G'day, Logan, I said,
changing my name
because this person
was no longer that left-right
reversed almost-replica,
but a stranger
standing in front of me.

I studied Logan closely,
but not overmuch,
for that would be rude.
He seemed pleasant enough,
lined face, careful hazel eyes,
sharp nose, similar clothes
to what I would wear,
which was a worrying start.

I extended my right hand
and Logan simultaneously
offered his left,
but no matter what we tried
a handshake seemed
impossible in this mirror world;
so, in the interests of courtesy,
we just waved (in sync),
and both smiled at the exact
same nanosecond, vanquishing
all that awkwardness.

Satisfied with our brief introduction,
we pivoted 180 and returned
to our respective worlds.

I'm sure he felt the way I did,
Logan, this man in the mirror,
that we could make a go of it;
indeed, we could get on very well.
Even at first glance, there was
so much in common between us.
Although, on reflection, that moustache
– *what* was he thinking!

The good thief

Softer than a meerkat's footfall, the thief drops from the window onto the bedroom floor. A young woman's troubled face glimmers in the faint light. Occasionally, she tosses and moans, her breathing ragged. He will need to be very, very quiet.

The thief glides closer, studies the loving couple on the bedside photo. And now there is one, he whispers.

Kneeling, he opens a small black bag, sweeps silent fingers above her forehead.

When she sleeps deeply, the thief closes his bag of stolen bad dreams, blows her a kiss, and smiles. He will fetch a pretty penny for his takings and is confident they will recycle to someone more deserving.

kismet
playing favourites
with people's lives…
drifting sunlight and clouds
patchwork the forest

Planetary conversations: Venus laments

You're not welcome here.

Fine. Watch me shine in your sky,
        the evening star, the early morning star;
only your moon out-lumens me at night.
Yes, you tracked my dotting the sun in transit,
        romanticised me, fantasised me
with your Lewis, Burroughs, Asimov.

But you called me Venus
        – so falsely. A goddess of love, beauty,
fertility, prosperity. How did you
have it so wrong? Here I hide
        with sorrowful eyes
behind clouds of yellow poison.

Now, you know better. Your *Magellan*
        swung around more than four earth years
and learned that I was, once,
a blue planet of rivers and oceans,
        and that your nomenclature
was not completely askew.

Now, you see the hard withering
        beneath my golden veil,
dry, desolate, scarred,
carbon dioxide levels beyond
        your nightmares, spewer
of greenhouse gases, sulphuric acid.

Does that sound like a welcome party?

Despite your pitiful attempts,
        I have crushed your probes
with my body of 90 atmospheres,
seared them at 462 degrees C;
        yet, you keep persisting.
Can you not take the hints?

You're not welcome here.

I still rage over the loss
        of what I used to be,
jealous of your Gaia's beauty
that taunts me with memories
        of when I made her look
like a total hag.

Yes, admire me from afar,
        easily my best aspect,
but fear me also,
because move on billions
        of years or so,
and I am your future.

Forget me, I am dead to you.

Barefoot

T
 h
  e
   r
   e
    is
     some
      thing
       primal
        wicked
         delightful
          about naked feet   nuzzling soft pile   toe-squeezing damp
           beachside sand   or jiggling at you
            from the other end   of your pool chair

Flying the colours

It's quirkily beautiful the way balloons disrupt Canberra's skyline, lifting into the air like liberated fridge magnets, stuttering the dawn-break blue with adverts, logos, architecture, a beagle, a floundering dinosaur. Even without binoculars, our crowd – scarfed, parka'd – can still spy the little people, shrinking rapidly as if they've eaten Alice's magic mushrooms. Their arms reach over the gondola edges, pointing out icons around Lake Burley Griffin.

we're losing friends
two migrating snipe
fade into the mist

Breakfast coffee and crepe aromas tease the nostrils of onlookers. A breeze quivers the flags of Old Parliament House. The rising sun joins the fleet, gilding their nylon gores and panels. Balloons scatter, early morning discussions complete, plans in place.

multi-coloured dreams
crowded my youthful sky
– not all blew away

A balloon wooooshes, suddenly spurts in height; but then, anyone would move if lit from beneath. Some linger low over the water, hovering near kayakers, exchanging greetings. The ninety-percent-inflated T-Rex wobbles on the lawn like a flatulent, overweight conqueror. Children and dogs weave in and out of the gaps around the gasping colossus like beetles on Benzedrine.

failed romance
a lyrebird loses his voice
mid-performance

Sipping coffee, we watch the giant beagle with its I-love-you-all grin drift past like a carnival float. Around us, ground staff begin to clean up and the crowd disperse. It's been such a great morning; most balloons have launched successfully – only a few have faltered under the conditions. But we'll all be here again tomorrow.

diamond drop earrings
plunge from the widow's ears –
a waterfall roars again

Slow Summer Night

Squeezing my clammy pillow in shared affliction,
I try the usual methods: counting kangaroos;
stretching and relaxing muscles;
reimagining stories; blanking the mind…
Yet, here I am. Humid pervasive warmth
enfolds me like a wool-lined straitjacket
soaked in steaming, stagnant water.

And, in this so-called silent night,
our air conditioner moans its last;
hordes of sleepless crickets knock
at the windows; a mischievous night owl
exults from a nearby tree;
the disharmonic steps of homebound partygoers
thump and trample the footpath, their laughter
travelling forever in the soggy air, ringing
in my ears like OD'd ghosts and ghouls
adance and acackle at Halloween.

Someplace in the darkness,
a mosquito's whine drums up the adrenaline.
I slide beneath my liquescent sheet,
not really the optimal location,
but when it's discomfort versus
being blood-sucked, well…

Even so, I almost drift into sublimity
until my partner turns over, muttering
noisily before her breathing pattern
settles from REM to non-REM.
I glare at her pale, inconsiderate
form flickering in the full moonlight
(which has successfully contrived to penetrate
the curtain's defences). Her completely
intolerable disregard for my insomnia
is surely a matter for marriage counselling!
For a moment, the temptation is there –
just a little nudge…

But I resolve to be patient, a martyr
to Chronos, who walks so slowly tonight.
If only the old reprobate were here right now,
I would kick the bearded wonder
right up his ample amplitude, chivvy him along,
advance the dawn, dispel this clammy torment,
and bring on the glorious noise of day.

Kandinsky – Composition VII (1913)

canvas beach backwash curiously
familiar glyphs of destruction
salvation apocalypse deliverance
merging entwining cascading
exploding maelstroms howling
for attention Babel discourses
roiling boiling lines criss-crossing
curves an insanity of contrasts
but look at the big picture
this is Wassily playing us
polyphonically his brush whips
up coloured coloratura orchestrated
extravaganza on full fortissimo
this is polychromatic opera
from the rhythmic reaches
of his synaesthetic imagination
and he's asking us to listen

Rebirth

Master artisan,
how I wish I were
a *real* antique,
not a human one…
where you could scrape

that old skin off,
that wrinkled old skin,
all those spots, freckles, warts
and unsightly protuberances.
You could putty me, nail me,
glue me, stain me, wax me,
polish me, rebuild me
inside to out;
replace historic parts
with new joints and fittings:
(oh joy, I shall leap tall buildings,
score impossible goals).

But, master artisan,
to extend this hypothetical
to my satisfaction,
some vintage character
must be left,
a patina of a life –
so don't, please don't,
mess with my mind
(although a gentle upgrade
would be nice). Preserve
my mortal memories
so that I can revisit and review
those errors, injustices, joys,
sadnesses, successes,
missed opportunities,
lovings, leavings…

Oh, master artisan,
if you could do all this for me,
how much better I would be
my second time around.

Acknowledgements

My thanks to the editors of the following publications where some of the poems in this collection first appeared (occasionally in different form):
Kindred Trees (2022): https://kindredtrees.com.au
Ribbons (2019, 2020, 2021, 2022)
Brushstrokes II, Ros Spencer Poetry Contest Anthology, 2020–21
Around the World: Landscapes & Cityscapes Anthology (Sweetycat Press, 2021)
Drifting Sands Haibun (2021)
Eucalypt (#27, #27, #29, #31, 2020–21)
Kokako (#32, #35, 2020–21)
Outer Space, Inner Minds, digital anthology (Interactive Publications, 2020)
Messages from the Embers: From Devastation to Hope: Australian Bushfire Poetry Anthology (Black Quill Press, 2020)
I Protest: Poems of Dissent anthology (Ginninderra Press, 2020)
These Tiny Threads Remind Me: Written in the Time of COVID-19 anthology (Nillumbik Council, 2020)
The Blue Nib (An Astráil, online, May 2020)
Lyrical Passion Poetry E-Zine (2020)
Harvesting Clouds anthology (Tram Stop Poets, Ginninderra Press, 2020)
The Other Bunny (2020)
Cattails (2019)
The Bamboo Hut (2019)
KYSO (KF-12, 2019)
MacQueen's Quinterly (Issue #1, 2019)
Poetry d'Amour Anthology 2019 (WA Poets Inc.)
Presence (#65, 2019)
SpeckLit (2016)
Bright Light Multimedia (Bright Light Café), 2007
'Walnut & Gold' edition (*The Wise Owl*, 2023)

About the author

Tony Steven Williams is a Canberra poet, short-fiction author and songwriter with many publications in journals, anthologies and magazines. Tony's poetic output is intentionally diverse both in form and material. An occasional speculative fiction piece is a frequent visitor. However, in all his work, environment and the human condition are very important to him. His debut poetry collection, *Sun and Moon, Light and Dark*, was published by Ginninderra Press in 2018.

www.ingramcontent.com/pod-product-compliance
Lightning Source LLC
Chambersburg PA
CBHW070307120526
44590CB00017B/2585